ACHIEVE 100 PLUS

Reading

REVISION

Laura Collinson

D1512955

RISING STARS

Acknowledgements

Rising Stars is grateful to the following schools who will be utilising Achieve to prepare their students for the National Tests: Chacewater Community Primary School, Cornwall; Coppice Primary School, Essex; Edgewood Primary School, Notts; Henwick Primary School, Eltham; Norwood Primary School, Southport; Sacred Heart Catholic Primary School, Manchester; Sunnyfields Primary School, Hendon; Tennyson Road Primary School, Luton.

Photo credits

Photos from iStock: p9 capybara © Volga2012; p10 loom bands © drpnncpp; p11 teapot © Belyaevskiy; p16 killer whale © Nerthuz; p20 bread mould © WildLivingArts; p21 sheep © GlobalP; p24 pigeon © soleg; p25 lit match © dja65; p28 theatre masks © pialhovik; p32 cola © Captainflash; p39 pizza © skodonnell; p41 UFO © homeworks255; p42 roller blades © Givaga; p43 fox © GlobalP; p44 boy © tap10; p47 horse © Kseniya Abramova; p48 rowing boat © AnetteAndersen; p48 abacus © Marjanneke; p49 owl © GlobalP; p51 train © jgorzynik; p52 cauldron © blackwaterimages; p53 watering can © YinYang; p54 Christmas tree © DNY59; p57 dragon head © Sylphe_7; p57 lamp © Gregory_DUBUS
Photos from Shutterstock: p15 chess pieces © pio3; p33 girl © PathDoc; p52 can-can dancer © ArtStudia Group

Text extracts

pp8, 47, 55 Alone on a Wide Sea, reprinted by permission of HarperCollins Publishers Ltd © 2006 Michael Morpurgo; pp9, 22, 23, 24 Journey to the River Sea by Eva Ibotson; p9 Crop circles article from First News; p10 Loom bands article from First News; pp11, 19 , 20, 21, 46, 48 The Orchard Book of Heroes & Villains by Tony Bradman & Tony Ross, published by Orchard Books, an Hachette UK Company; p11 The Hollow Land by Jane Gardam © Europa Editions; p12 The Lion, the Witch and the Wardrobe by C.S. Lewis copyright © C.S. Lewis Pte. Ltd. 1950. Extracts reprinted by permission; p13 The Iron Man by Ted Hughes, Faber & Faber 1986; pp14, 54 Santa and Christmas articles from Families Chiltern magazine © Gavin Thomas; p16 Map of the UK and Ships article from First News; p19 Swimming article/extract © Primary Times; p20 Excerpt from The Shaman's Apprentice: A Tale of the Amazon's Forest by Lynne Cherry and Mark J Plotkin. Text copyright © 1998 by Lynne Cherry and Mark J. Plotkin, reprinted by permission of Houghton Mifflin Harcourt Publishing Company. All rights reserved; p21 Halloween article from First News; p23 The Ship Between the Worlds by Julia Golding © Oxford University Press; p24 Text © 1992 Pigeon Summer by Ann Turnbull, reproduced by permission of Walker Books Ltd, London SE11 5HJ www.walker.co.uk; p25 The Railway Children by E Nesbit; Farm Boy, reprinted by permission of HarperCollins Publishers Ltd © 2011 Michael Morpurgo; p26 Troops article from First News; p28 Anne Marie Scanlon on behalf of Primary Times Magazine 2014; p29 Text © 2001 Michael Rosen. From Shakespeare, His Work & His World by Michael Rosen, illustrated by Robert Ingpen, reproduced by permission of Walker Books Ltd, London SE11 5HJ www.walker.co.uk; Visitor information leaflet © Drayton Manor Theme Park; p30 A Spell to Cure Sorrow and Create Joy by Clare Bevan; p31 Time © John Foster 2009; Left Out © Celia Warren, first published in Feelings Poems – John Foster, OUP, 1998; p32 Wanted! by Richard Caley; Things I'd do if it weren't for Mum by Tony Mitton, published by Macmillan's Children's Books; p33 Rebecca from Cautionary Tales by Hilaire Belloc, reprinted by permission of Peters Fraser & Dunlop (www.petersfraserdunlop.com) on behalf of the Estate of Hilaire Belloc; p34 The Secret Garden by Frances Hodgson Burnett; pp38, 57 How to Train Your Dragon by Cressida Cowell, published by Little, Brown and Company & Hachette Children's Group; p39 Pizza by funguerilla.com; The Water Babies © Charles Kingsley; p40 Top 10 reasons to visit the Eden Project © The Eden Project; p41 Crop circles article from First News; Bicycle © Cris Woodford by kind permission of explainthatstuff.com; p42 Maturity Poem by Dajanay; p43 Suzie & June © EreadingWorksheets.com; p44 Billy Doesn't Like School by Paul Cookson; pp48, 49 Bad Kids by Tony Robinson published by Macmillan's Children's Books; p49 Extract from Tom's Midnight Garden by Philippa Pearce (OUP, 2008), copyright © Oxford University Press 1958, reproduced by permission of Oxford University Press; p50 The Highway Man from The Society of Authors as the Literary Representative of the Estate of Alfred Noyes; p51 From a Railway Carriage by Robert Louis Stevenson; p52 Macbeth by William Shakespeare; A Twister for Two Tongues reprinted by permission of © Cynthia Rider; p53 Ernie – A Cautionary Tale, © John Foster 2009 from 'The Works 8' (Macmillan), included by permission of John Foster; p56 Differences between toads and frogs from allaboutfrogs.org by Dorota; p57 Goodnight Mister Tom by Michelle Magorian, Puffin 2010, reproduced by permission of Penguin Books Ltd

Every effort has been made to trace all copyright holders, but if any have been inadvertently overlooked, the Publishers will be pleased to make the necessary arrangements at the first opportunity.

Although every effort has been made to ensure that website addresses are correct at time of going to press, Rising Stars cannot be held responsible for the content of any website mentioned in this book. It is sometimes possible to find a relocated web page by typing in the address of the home page for a website in the URL window of your browser.

Hachette UK's policy is to use papers that are natural, renewable and recyclable products and made from wood grown in sustainable forests. The logging and manufacturing processes are expected to conform to the environmental regulations of the country of origin.

ISBN: 978 1 78339 547 7

© Rising Stars UK Ltd 2015

First published in 2015 by Rising Stars UK Ltd, part of Hodder Education, an Hachette UK Company

Carmelite House

50 Victoria Embankment

London EC4Y 0DZ

Reprinted 2015

www.risingstars-uk.com

Author: Laura Collinson

Author (pages 12–17, 34–45): Ione Branton

Series Editor: Helen Lewis

Accessibility Reviewer: Vivien Kilburn

Publishers: Kate Jamieson and Laura White

Project Manager: Estelle Lloyd

Editorial: Sarah Davies, Rachel Evans, Anne Kilraine, Fiona Leonard

Cover design: Burville-Riley Partnership

Illustrations by John Storey, Pen and Ink Book Company Ltd

Text design and typeset by the Pen and Ink Book Company Ltd

Printed by Craft Print Pte Limited, Singapore

A catalogue record for this title is available from the British Library.

Contents

Welcome to Achieve Key Stage 2 Reading Revision Book 100+

Well done for completing Achieve Revision Book 100, revising everything you need to achieve the expected scaled score of 100 in the Key Stage 2 Reading test. You are now ready for the next step. In this book you will find key information and activities for more practice and to help you achieve 100+. You will look again at some of the same key knowledge that was in Achieve 100, but you will use it to tackle trickier questions and apply it in more complex ways.

About the Key Stage 2 Reading National Test

The test will take place in the summer term in Year 6. It will be done in your school and will be marked by examiners – not by your teacher.

In the test you will be given a booklet containing a range of texts and another booklet for your answers. The texts will be from a range of fiction, non-fiction and poetry. The first text will be the easiest and the last text will be the most challenging. The texts and questions will be very similar to the texts that you have been reading in school. You will have one hour to read the texts and complete the answer booklet.

The test is worth a total of 50 marks.

- Some questions ask you to find the answer in the text. These questions are usually worth 1 mark. These make up 44–66 % of the marks.
- Some questions ask you to write a short answer. These questions are usually worth 2 marks. They make up 20–40 % of the marks.
- Other questions ask you to write a longer answer. These are worth 3 marks. They make up 6–24 % of the marks.

Test techniques

Before the test

- Try to revise little and often, rather than in long sessions.
- Choose a time of day when you are not tired or hungry.
- Choose somewhere quiet so you can focus.
- Revise with a friend. You can encourage and learn from each other.
- Read the 'Top tips' throughout this book to remind you of important points in answering test questions.
- Use the advice given in this book when you are reading your own reading book. Ask yourself some of the questions as you read along.
- KEEP READING all kinds of non-fiction, fiction and poetry texts.

During the test

- READ THE QUESTION AND READ IT AGAIN.
- If you find a question difficult to answer, move on; you can always come back to it later.
- Always answer a multiple-choice question. If you really can't work out the answer, have a guess.
- Check to see how many marks a question is worth. Have you written enough to 'earn' those marks in your answer?
- Read the question again after you have answered it. Check you have done what the question asked you to do.
- If you have any time left at the end, go back to the questions you have missed. If you really do not know the answers, make guesses.

Where to get help

- Pages 8–57 will help you develop the skills you need to achieve a scaled score of more than 100 in the test.
- Page 58 contains a glossary to help you understand key terms about writing, reading and grammar.
- Pages 59–62 provide the answers to the 'Try this' questions.

How to use this book

1 **_Introduction_** – This section introduces each assessable element so you know what you need to achieve.

2 **_What you need to know_** – Important facts about the assessable elements are given in this section. Read them carefully. Words in bold are key words and those in lilac are also defined in the glossary at the back of the book.

3 **_Text examples_** – These are short extracts from the types of text you can expect to find in the Key Stage 2 Reading National Test.

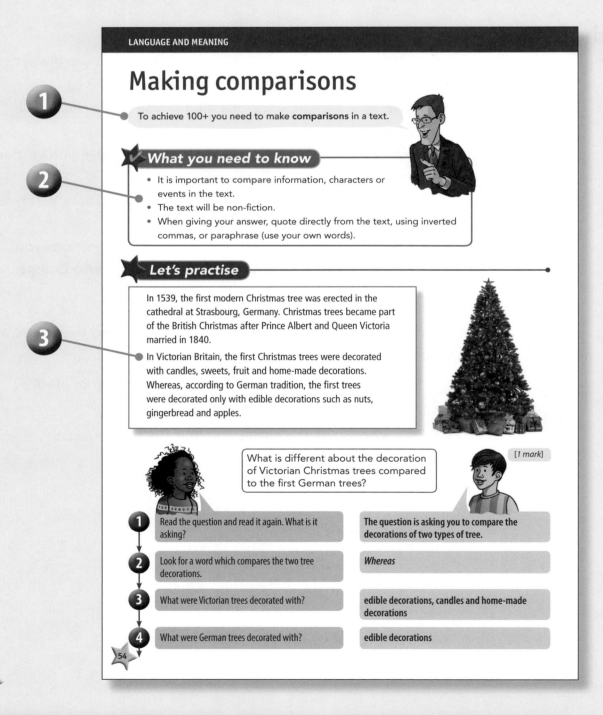

LANGUAGE AND MEANING

Making comparisons

1

To achieve 100+ you need to make **comparisons** in a text.

2

What you need to know

- It is important to compare information, characters or events in the text.
- The text will be non-fiction.
- When giving your answer, quote directly from the text, using inverted commas, or paraphrase (use your own words).

Let's practise

3

In 1539, the first modern Christmas tree was erected in the cathedral at Strasbourg, Germany. Christmas trees became part of the British Christmas after Prince Albert and Queen Victoria married in 1840.

In Victorian Britain, the first Christmas trees were decorated with candles, sweets, fruit and home-made decorations. Whereas, according to German tradition, the first trees were decorated only with edible decorations such as nuts, gingerbread and apples.

What is different about the decoration of Victorian Christmas trees compared to the first German trees? [1 mark]

1 Read the question and read it again. What is it asking?	The question is asking you to compare the decorations of two types of tree.
2 Look for a word which compares the two tree decorations.	*Whereas*
3 What were Victorian trees decorated with?	edible decorations, candles and home-made decorations
4 What were German trees decorated with?	edible decorations

54

4 *Let's practise* – This gives an example question for you to read through. Follow the steps carefully and work through the example.

 5 *Try this* – Practise answering the questions for yourself.

 6 *Glossary* – A glossary for each practice test is provided to help with tricky words.

 7 *Top tips* – These hints help you to do your best. Use them well.

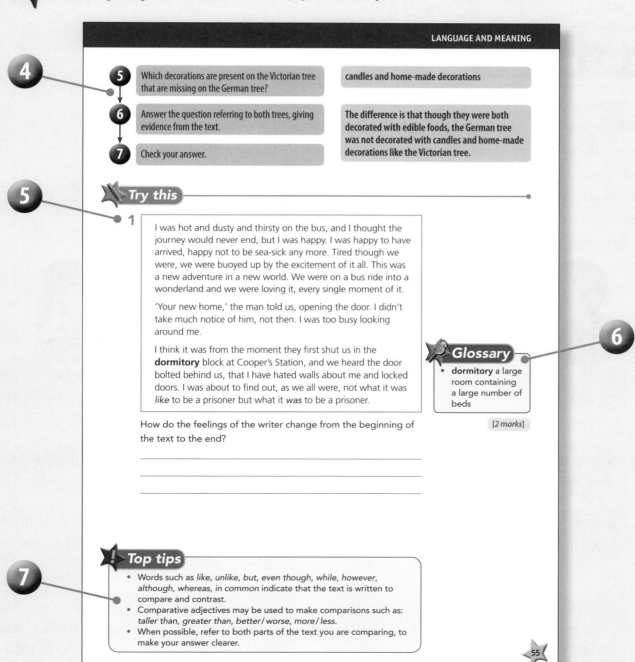

LANGUAGE AND MEANING

4

5 Which decorations are present on the Victorian tree that are missing on the German tree?

candles and home-made decorations

6 Answer the question referring to both trees, giving evidence from the text.

The difference is that though they were both decorated with edible foods, the German tree was not decorated with candles and home-made decorations like the Victorian tree.

7 Check your answer.

5

Try this

1

> I was hot and dusty and thirsty on the bus, and I thought the journey would never end, but I was happy. I was happy to have arrived, happy not to be sea-sick any more. Tired though we were, we were buoyed up by the excitement of it all. This was a new adventure in a new world. We were on a bus ride into a wonderland and we were loving it, every single moment of it.
>
> 'Your new home,' the man told us, opening the door. I didn't take much notice of him, not then. I was too busy looking around me.
>
> I think it was from the moment they first shut us in the **dormitory** block at Cooper's Station, and we heard the door bolted behind us, that I have hated walls about me and locked doors. I was about to find out, as we all were, not what it was *like* to be a prisoner but what it *was* to be a prisoner.

6

Glossary

• **dormitory** a large room containing a large number of beds

How do the feelings of the writer change from the beginning of the text to the end?

_____

_____

_____

[2 marks]

7

Top tips

• Words such as *like, unlike, but, even though, while, however, although, whereas, in common* indicate that the text is written to compare and contrast.
• Comparative adjectives may be used to make comparisons such as: *taller than, greater than, better / worse, more / less.*
• When possible, refer to both parts of the text you are comparing, to make your answer clearer.

Explaining the meaning of words in context

To achieve 100+ you need to explain the meaning of a word or phrase in **context**.

✔ *What you need to know*

- Some words or phrases can mean different things depending on the **context** in which they are written.
- It is important to relate the meaning of a given word or phrase to the text as a whole.
- Write quotations in **quotation marks**.

Let's practise

Evening was coming on by the time we got to Cooper's Station, but we could still see enough. We could see it was a place on its own, way out in the bush, and we could tell it was a farm. I mean you could smell it straightaway, the moment we clambered down off the bus. There were huge sheds all around, and you could hear cattle moving and shifting around inside. And from further away in the gloom there was the sound of a running creek, and ducks quacking raucously.

Explain why the word *gloom* is an appropriate word to describe the time of day.

[*1 mark*]

1 Read the question and read it again. What is it asking?

The question is asking why *gloom* has been used to describe the way it looks at a particular time of day.

2 Find the word *gloom* in the text. Read the whole sentence. Is the definition given to you?

No. I will find other phrases that discuss the time of day: *Evening was coming on*

3 How does *evening* and the ability to see relate to how it looks at this time of day?

It tells you it was getting dark. You may find it difficult to see in the dark. *Dark* is a synonym for *gloom*.

4 Use the clues and what you know about the time of day to answer the question. Use evidence from the text if it supports your answer. Then, check your answer.

Gloom is an appropriate word to use because it is a synonym for *dark*, but not so dark that you can't see. The text says that it is evening, the time when it would be getting dark.

 **Try this**

1

Once a litter of **capybaras** lumbered after their mother and they were close enough to see their funny snouts and sandy fur. Once they passed a tree whose roots had been killed by the rise of the water, and its bare branches were full of scarlet and blue parakeets which flew up, screeching, when the boat came past. And once Maia saw a grey log lying in the shallows which suddenly came to life. 'Oh look,' she said, 'A croc – I mean an alligator!'

Glossary

• **capybara** a South American mammal that resembles a long-legged guinea pig

And once Maia saw a grey log lying in the shallows… [1 mark]
Why has the word *shallows* been used to describe the river?

_____

_____

2

In August, 2014, an incredible crop circle was discovered in farmer Christoph Huttner's wheat field by a hot air balloonist flying over the stretch of land, near Bavaria in southern Germany. The unusual thing is that there wasn't a trace of the circle the day before – it mysteriously appeared overnight!

Since its discovery, hundreds upon hundreds of people have gathered at the site to witness the creation with their own eyes. The crop circle in Huttner's field is 75 m (264 ft) in diameter and it's big enough to allow visitors to walk through it like a maze. But what caused it? Huttner believes students on their summer holidays are responsible for the creation and has not yet decided whether or not he will keep the crop circle as an attraction in his field.

Crop circles commonly make headlines because of the mystery attached to them. They are created by flattening crops in fields to form a large, often circular, symbol or pattern visible from the sky. Often, the people that make them never reveal themselves, which adds an obvious element of mystery to their creation.

Explain why the words *creation* and *created* have been used to describe crop circles. [1 mark]

_____

_____

3

> Without warning, Durga pounced! She attacked Hydra with her trusty sword and protective shield, but Hydra quickly wound her four necks tight around Durga's slim body. Using her wit, Durga made herself invisible and squeezed out of the demon's firm grasp. Suddenly, the snake monster swung round, swiping her tail around the dimly-lit cave, smashing the calcified stalactites into the fetid water below. Silently, Hydra slithered beneath the stinking surface and looked up to see the whereabouts of Durga.
>
> After what seemed like an age, the image of Durga appeared, standing on the rim of the foul-smelling water's edge. Without warning, the snake demon pounced, noxious blood dripping from her tightened mouth. As quick as a flash, Durga brought out her torch of fire and pushed it into each of Hydra's eight menacing eyes. She was blinded! She was furious! She couldn't see. Hydra let out a monstrous ear piercing scream! But it was too late ... Durga sliced off each of Hydra's heads. They plunged one by one into the disgusting water and slowly sank to the bottom ...

Why is *fetid* an appropriate word to describe the water in the cave? [1 mark]

_____

_____

4

> The recent boom in loom bands means there are millions of colourful elastic bands in homes across the UK, but just what happens to them when they're no longer wanted?
>
> Experts have warned that the elastic bands could be a problem for the environment as they can't be recycled.
>
> The bands have become a huge craze, with millions being sold across the world.
>
> However, as they are made from plastic or a type of silicone, the bands don't break down naturally. This means that if large numbers are thrown away, they may become a problem for the environment.
>
> There are also concerns that discarded bands could be dangerous if they are swallowed by pets such as cats or dogs, or by marine life if the bands end up in the sea.
>
> Experts have said that if the loom band craze continues, schemes may need to be put in place to deal with unwanted bands. In the meantime, use your loom bands creatively to make sure they don't end up in the bin!

a) **Find** and **copy** a phrase that shows loom bands have a dangerous effect on nature. [1 mark]

_____

b) Explain why the phrase you chose is appropriate to describe loom bands. [1 mark]

_____

_____

5

On the second day of the voyage a wild hurricane blew out of the Atlantic, and the howling winds quickly drove the ship so far off course, the captain had no idea where they were. The sails were ripped from the spars, and the ship was tossed like a toy on colossal waves. Robinson felt horribly sick, and grimly held onto a mast. Suddenly there was a CRASH! and the ship juddered to a halt, its masts swaying, its timbers groaning as if the vessel was in agony. By now it was night, and the winds were wilder than ever.

'We've struck a reef!' yelled the captain at last. 'We're stuck on it too, and the sea will soon smash the hull to pieces … ABANDON SHIP!'

The crew wrestled the lifeboat into the sea, and they all jumped into it. They rowed away, hoping to find land.

The crew wrestled the lifeboat into the sea…　　　　　[1 mark]

Why is *wrestled* an appropriate word to describe how the crew got the lifeboat into the sea?

_____

_____

6

The tea when it came was very ample. But rather dry. Plate after plate the bristle woman brought. Different kinds of pale, heavy cake lay on these. All the things looked rather old though they were definitely home-made. They had been built, like the bristle woman herself, to last.

The butter was marg.

A giant pot of tea arrived.

Harry asked again for a glass of water. Or orange.

'Milk,' said the bristle woman and brought milk and went away again.

Harry (who was always good) – said in a minute, 'I can't drink it.'

'Oh Harry!' said his mother.

'It tastes of meat.'

'Don't be silly. Let me try.'

It tasted of meat.

The tea when it came was very ample.　　　　　[1 mark]

Explain what the word *ample* tells you about how much tea came.

_____

_____

 **Top tips**

- Look for the definition of the word nearby in the text. Words and phrases including *like, including, such as, known as, meaning* or *which* may help you to find the definition.
- Use your own knowledge of synonyms for the given word or look for synonyms in the text.
- The more detail you provide in an explanation, the more marks you will be awarded. If the answer box contains more than one line, give a more detailed answer.

Retrieving information and identifying key details

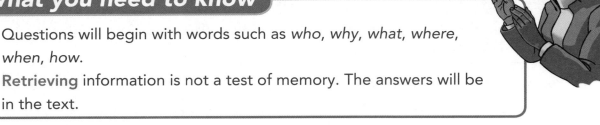

To achieve 100+ you need to **find** and **record** details and information from the text.

✔ What you need to know

- Questions will begin with words such as *who, why, what, where, when, how.*
- **Retrieving** information is not a test of memory. The answers will be in the text.

★ Let's practise

… so that in a very few minutes everyone was drawing up their stools (it was all three-legged stools in the Beavers' house except for Mrs Beaver's own special rocking-chair beside the fire) and preparing to enjoy themselves. There was a jug of creamy milk for the children (Mr Beaver stuck to beer) and a great big lump of deep yellow butter in the middle of the table from which everyone took as much as he wanted to go with his potatoes, and all the children thought – and I agree with them – that there's nothing to beat good freshwater fish if you eat it when it has been alive half an hour ago and has come out of the pan half a minute ago.

Circle the correct option to complete each sentence below.

a) The rocking-chair was used by… *[1 mark]*

| Mr Beaver. | the children. | the oldest child. | Mrs Beaver. |

b) The children took as much as they wanted of… *[1 mark]*

| potatoes. | butter. | milk. | fish. |

1 Read the first question and read it again. What is it asking?

It is asking you to choose the correct option to complete the sentence 'The rocking-chair was used by …'.

2 Read the text and find whose rocking-chair it was.

It says they all sat on stools except for Mrs Beaver's own special rocking-chair.

3 Read the choices you have and choose the correct one.

It is the last choice: Mrs Beaver. Circle Mrs Beaver.

4 Read the second question and find the answer in the text.

It says 'the children took as much as they wanted of ...'. In the text it says there was *a great big lump of deep yellow butter from which everyone took as much as he wanted to go with his potatoes.*

5 Read the choices you have and choose the correct one.

It is the second choice: butter. Circle butter.

6 Check your answers.

Try this

1

> Next morning, it landed – on Australia.
>
> Barrrump!
>
> The shock of its landing rolled round the Earth like an earthquake, spilling teacups in London, jolting pictures off walls in California, cracking statues off their pedestals in Russia. The thing had actually landed – and it was a terrific dragon.
>
> Terribly black, terribly scaly, terribly knobbly, terribly horned, terribly hairy, terribly clawed, terribly fanged, with vast indescribably terrible eyes, each one as big as Switzerland.

Circle the correct option to complete each sentence below.

a) The dragon landed on the Earth... [1 mark]

heavily.   carefully.   briefly.   quietly.

b) The dragon is likened to... [1 mark]

a country.   an earthquake.   a picture.   a teacup.

c) Statues fell off their pedestals in... [1 mark]

California.   Switzerland.   Russia.   Australia.

d) The dragon's eyes were... [1 mark]

small.   shiny.   green.   huge.

2

> **270 AD**   Santa is one of the most **evocative** images of Christmas. But there were several forerunners to this jolly gentleman with a snowy-white beard. Perhaps the most famous was Nikolaos of Myra, also known as Saint Nicholas, celebrated for his kindness to children and generosity to the poor.
>
> **17th century**   The first recipes for plum pudding – the ancestor of the modern Christmas pudding – appear. According to tradition, puddings should contain 13 ingredients, representing Christ and the 12 apostles.
>
> **18th century**   The British tradition of kissing under a sprig of mistletoe as a pledge of marriage begins. At Christmas it was believed a girl standing beneath mistletoe could not refuse anyone wishing to kiss her.
>
> **19th century**   The legend begins, claiming that Father Christmas lives at the North Pole, with a large number of magical elves to help wrap and distribute the presents, as well as some flying reindeer.

Glossary
- **evocative** memorable

Circle the correct option to complete each sentence below.

a) Saint Nicholas was celebrated for being…   [1 mark]

   secretive.   generous.   jolly.   famous.

b) The tradition of kissing under the mistletoe started in…   [1 mark]

   270AD.   the 17th century.   the 18th century.   the 19th century.

c) Christ and the 12 apostles are represented in…   [1 mark]

   the pudding ingredients.   the pledge of marriage.   the presents.   the sprig of mistletoe.

d) If you are standing under the mistletoe you are not allowed to refuse…   [1 mark]

   a present.   a kiss.   a pudding.   marriage.

Top tips
- Put a circle around only one of the choices.
- Do not write anything else on the answer sheet.
- Read the question sentence together with your choice to check it makes sense.

3

George was hesitant to let Harry borrow his antique chess set. Though it wasn't worth much money, the set had been in the family for a long time and was irreplaceable. But Harry was persistent and asked his brother time and again to borrow the set. Unrelenting, George would not share.

Harry was determined to show George just what he thought. He ran upstairs to George's room and looked around. 'I'll show him. Where shall I start?' he thought to himself. With one swipe, Harry knocked all George's aircraft models off the shelf. George had spent hours gluing them together to showcase as a set. Now they were in wooden shards on the bedroom floor.

Not content with his destruction, Harry continued to turn over the mattress on the bed. His face was red, and he wiped drips of sweat from his head with the back of his hand, onto George's best sweatshirt. The tirade continued; pens on the floor, clothes in a pile, homework ripped to shreds. After what seemed like seconds, he stopped for breath and looked up at the door!

Using the information in the text, tick ✔ **true** or **false** in the table below.

[1 mark]

	True	False
The chess set had been owned by the family for a long time.		
George shared the chess set with Harry.		
George's aircraft models were made of metal.		
Harry tore up George's homework.		

! Top tips

- In True / False questions use ✔ to show your answer.
- Only tick one box in each row.

4

1 Dundee
Sports centre site revealed

Dundee's Caird Park is to become the home of a new £10m regional sports centre. The facility will be open to professional athletes and the general public.

2 Newcastle
Strictly to the stage

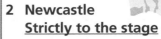

TV's Craig Revel Horwood will be taking to the stage next year as villain Miss Hannigan in a production of the musical *Annie*.

3 Cardiff
Charity bike ride

Local cyclists rode from Boston to New York recently, raising £600,000 for Cardiff's Velindre Cancer Centre. The team covered 515km in their epic two-week-long feat.

4 London
Train delay thief jailed

A burglar who caused a whopping 17 hours of rail delays by hiding in a tree overlooking train tracks has been jailed for 18 months. Police eventually captured the crook after a 17-hour stand-off.

Using the information on the map, tick ✔ **true** or **false** in the table below.   [*1 mark*]

	True	False
A new sports centre will be built in Cardiff.		
The cyclists who rode from Boston to New York raised £600,000.		
The burglar who caused the train delay has been jailed for 17 months.		
Craig Revel Horwood will star in *Annie*.		

5

Ships are being offered money to lower their speeds off the coast of California, in the hope it will protect more whales.

Whales may be the oceans' giants, but even they are tiny compared to the giant ships that sail our seas.

The Santa Barbara Channel, off the coast of California, is home to many endangered species of whale. It is also one of the busiest channels in the world, allowing ships access to ports like Los Angeles and Long Beach.

This aquatic motorway is so busy that it means bad news for the whales who live there. If they are hit by one of these larger ships, the impact can cause serious injuries, if not kill them.

In a bid to reduce these collisions and protect more whales, six large shipping companies are being asked to slow their speeds down as part of a test.

Using the information in the text, complete the table below about the shipping trial.

[2 marks]

Which **two** ports are the ships in the Santa Barbara Channel using?	
What is the danger whales face from the ships?	
What are the shipping companies being asked to do in the test?	

Summarising main ideas

To achieve 100+ you need to **summarise** the **main ideas** in a text and identify the **key details** that support these ideas.

 What you need to know

- Within a text, every paragraph has a key concept or **main idea**. The main ideas in a text are the most important pieces of information.
- The **key details** in a text are the words, phrases or sentences that communicate the main ideas.
- When identifying key details you can quote directly from the text, using inverted commas, or **paraphrase** (use your own words).

Let's practise

Next came the queen, in the sixty-sixth year of her age, as we were told, very majestic; her face, oblong, fair but wrinkled; her eyes small yet black and pleasant; her nose a little hooked; her lips narrow and her teeth black.

She had in her ears two pearls with very rich drops; she wore false hair, and that red; upon her head she had a small crown. She had on a necklace of exceeding fine jewels; her hands were small, her fingers long, and her stature neither tall nor low.

Summarise the main idea in this text in **one** sentence.

[1 mark]

1 Read the question and read it again. What is it asking?

The question is asking you to summarise the text by stating the main idea.

2 Read the text again. What is the first thing it tells you about the queen?

It tells you how old she is.

3 Identify key details to describe the queen's features that may be related to her age.

face, oblong, fair but wrinkled; small eyes; narrow lips; black teeth; *false hair*

4 Does information about her jewels or fingers relate to her age?

No. It tells you what jewellery she wore.

5 Do not add information or your opinion. What is the main idea the text tells you about the queen? Then, check your answer.

The text tells us that the queen is ageing, but still a very impressive figure.

18

 **Try this**

1

'Stop, I've seen enough!' Philip growled at last. Alexander met his father's one-eyed gaze and waited for the verdict. 'Not bad …' said Philip, and Alexander smiled. Philip hadn't finished, though. 'But not wonderful, either. And I was better when I was your age. A lot better.'

Then he dug his heels in his horse's flanks and cantered off across the courtyard without so much as a backward glance, his men clattering along after him. Alexander watched them go, his smile now a grimace, the sweat cooling on his skin. A cloud passed over the sun and he shivered.

Alexander swallowed his disappointment that time. Philip came to see him train every day and Alexander tried even harder to impress him. But his nerves made him clumsy and Philip was quick to tell him so.

Explain what the relationship is like between Alexander and his father, Philip. [2 marks]
Include **two** key details to support your explanation.

_____

_____

_____

2

There are so many great things to say about swimming that it's hard to know where to start. For 'sporty' types, swimming can be one of the most competitive and wide-ranging arenas of sport there is from sprints to marathons; swimming can stretch even the most able of athletes. For the less sporty, swimming can be a great way to pass the time. You can swim solo or you can compete. You can swim fast, slow, with technique or just splashing about. Swimming is that rare thing in sports, and even in life; it can be all things to all people. You don't have to be coordinated, you don't have to be a certain weight, you don't have to spend money on expensive equipment and you don't have to pass a test to get into a pool.

Write a headline for this text. [2 marks]
Explain why you have chosen this headline.
Use the text to support your answer.

_____

_____

_____

3

Alfred sighed and stared into the flames and wondered for the thousandth time what he should do now. He felt a complete fool. Guthrum's trick had worked and it seemed that his Viking warriors had won. The Saxon army was scattered, their king, Alfred, a **fugitive**, hunted throughout the land that had been ruled by his family for generations. Maybe he should just give up.

Perhaps he could join a monastery. At least there he might be able to read. He reached beneath his damp cloak and pulled out a small book, the only one he had been able to bring with him from the palace. It was a book of old poems, tales of heroes fighting monsters, the last stands of warriors against overwhelming odds and sad stories of loss and longing. Alfred sat reading, deeply engrossed, and didn't notice the smell of burning bread that gradually began to fill the hut. But the old woman did.

She dashed over to the hearth and pulled the blackened loaves out of the ashes. But it was too late. They were ruined.

Glossary

- **fugitive** a person who is in hiding or running away from something

In **one** sentence, use key details to explain the main reason why the loaves burned.

[1 mark]

_____

_____

4

All of the world's cultures use plants and other growing things as medicines. In our industrialised society, most of the medicines we use are manufactured from synthetic chemicals based on **compounds** found in natural products.

Aspirin, for example, is based on a chemical that came from willow bark; codeine in cough syrup was derived from chemicals in the opium poppy; and penicillin was first extracted from a bread mould. In the more remote corners of the world, such as in the jungles of the Amazon, people have always used the forest as their medicine cabinet. For thousands of years, **shamans** have passed on information about the healing properties of rainforest plants from one generation to the next.

Write a suitable title for this text.
Explain your choice, using key details from the text.

[2 marks]

Glossary

- **compounds** mixtures
- **shaman** a person who uses ancient healing traditions for cures

_____

_____

_____

_____

5

By the early 800s, the Christian religion had almost taken over Celtic land and introduced a day known as All Souls Day to their calendar on 2nd November, the day after the Celtic New Year. This day, which had very similar traditions to the Celts' **Samhain**, was soon called All-Hallows Eve and then, eventually, Halloween.

As with most things, these traditions evolved, adapted and spread from people to people over time. The Celts controlled areas of Ireland and Europe when Samhain was celebrated and as it grew and became reshaped by different groups and religions, it reached the west coast of America. So, Halloween took quite a while, hundreds of years in fact, to evolve into the night of frights and frolics it's famous for today.

Glossary

- **Samhain** an ancient Celtic festival, celebrating the arrival of the new year on 1st November

Write a title for this text.   [1 mark]
Explain your choice, using key details from the text to support your answer.

_____

_____

_____

6

David's job was to look after the family's sheep and he had just brought the flock in from the hills for the night. 'I definitely want to go and face the Philistines too,' said David to his brothers and father. The Philistines were a tribe of fierce fighters who were at war with David's tribe, the Israelites.

'Don't be stupid,' said his oldest brother, Eliab. 'It will be men's work, David – proper fighting, not some pretend adventure for a boy.'

'I'm not a boy,' said David, 'I'm nearly grown up and I'm tired of you lot treating me like a child. You'll let me go, Father, won't you?'

Jesse had always had a soft spot for his youngest son and sometimes indulged his wishes. But on this occasion Jesse agreed with his first-born.

'No, I'm sorry, David,' he said. 'Eliab is right. You're just not old enough to be a warrior.'

What is the main idea in this text?   [2 marks]
Explain using evidence from the text to support your answer.

_____

_____

_____

! Top tips

- Use **skimming** and **scanning** to locate key details.
- Underline and group together key details, including information that is repeated within a paragraph or across paragraphs.

Explaining inferences in fiction

To achieve 100+ you need to make **inferences** and **deductions** in fiction, drawing on evidence from the text and justifying your views.

✔ What you need to know

- Writers often use clues to imply meaning about characters or events in fiction texts.
- Good readers:
  - make **deductions** and draw conclusions about a character's feelings based on their speech and actions;
  - support their **inferences** with a precise explanation of the evidence;
  - draw conclusions about the plot based on past events.
- If quoting directly from the text, write quotations in quotation marks.

★ Let's practise

Maia put her head round the door. In the corridor, wearing a dressing gown and a turban to protect her hair, was Mrs Carter. She had the flit gun in her hand and was carefully squirting every nook and cranny with insect-killer. Then she disappeared into the cloakroom, fetched a broom, and began to thump and bang on the ceiling to get rid of possible spiders. Next came a bucket full of disinfectant and a mop with which she squelched across the tiled floor – and all the time she muttered, 'Out!' or 'That will settle you!' to the insects that she thought might be there.

What impression of Mrs Carter does the writer give? Explain your answer as fully as you can.

[2 marks]

1 Read the question and read it again. What is it asking?

The question is asking you to explain what Mrs Carter is like.

2 How does the text describe Mrs Carter's character?

The text describes her through her actions.

3 Identify the main point about the actions of Mrs Carter.

Mrs Carter is doing everything she can to get rid of insects.

4 Find evidence to prove your main point.

She squirts places with an insect-killer. She bangs on the ceiling. She uses disinfectant on the floor. She tells the insects to get out.

5 What does this tell you about Mrs Carter? Answer with an explanation of your inference with evidence from the text.

The writer is trying to say that Mrs Carter is a very determined woman. This is shown by the way that she disinfects and cleans a lot to kill insects. She bangs on the ceiling to get rid of spiders and talks to them, muttering *Out* and *That will settle you*.

6 Check your answer.

 **Try this**

1

There were a lot of people in Manaus who lived like princes. But not the Carters. Because to get the juice from the rubber trees you need Indians who know the forest and understand the trees. And Indians are proud people who have their own lives. If you treat them like slaves they don't revolt or go on strike; they simply melt back into the forest, join their tribes and disappear.

This is what had happened to the Indians which the Carters had employed. Every month Mr Carter had lost some of his work force, and far from making his fortune, he was getting poorer and poorer.

What can you infer from the text about Mr Carter's attitude towards the Indians? Explain your answer giving evidence from the text.

[3 marks]

_____

_____

2

'School!' his mother called from downstairs. 'Get a move on, David!'

Reluctantly, he put down the triangular patch of white cotton he had intended for a sail at the prow of his ship. He wished he could stay all day with his model in its glass cocoon but he knew from experience that his mother would make him face school – and Rick – whatever excuse he invented. He'd previously tried claiming to be ill with most infectious diseases known to mankind, ranging from flu to (on one particularly desperate occasion) plague, but somehow, after clucking sympathetically, his mother always prescribed breakfast and a bracing walk to school as the cure. Heaven help him if he ever was really sick.

What conclusions had David come to about what his mother's decision would be? Justify your answer with evidence from the text.

[1 mark]

_____

_____

3

The hut was just as Bernard Taverner had left it when he went out with an Indian friend to look for the blue water-lily whose leaves were used as a painkiller. His collecting boxes and specimen jars, his plant press and dissecting kit and microscope, were all stacked neatly on his work table. His carpentry tools were hung carefully on the wooden wall; on the other side of the hut was the tackle for the boat. The khaki sheet still lay folded on his hammock as though he expected to return to sleep that night.

And in shelves made from palm-wood planks were rows of old books – books on natural history, books on exploration and all the well-known classics.

What might Mr Taverner's occupation be?
Give examples from the text to support your answer.

[2 marks]

_____

_____

4

'My pigeons, you've cooked my pigeons!'

'Your father's pigeons,' her mother corrected her. She was prepared, ready for battle.

'We've had pigeon before,' said Mum calmly. 'Your dad doesn't give them an old age pension, does he, when they're past it? They go in the pot.'

'But Dad chooses. Dad decides,' said Mary.

'And Dad's not here.'

'You killed Ruby,' Mary's voice rose. 'Ruby!'

'I just took the nearest.'

'But Ruby had a squeaker, a baby. And you killed her.'

'I've got a baby too. Your sister, Doreen. Isn't she more important than a pigeon?'

Her logic infuriated Mary. 'You'd no right! No right to take them!'

Her mother turned on her. 'I had every right, my girl! It's my job to feed this family, my job is to find food. Your sister has the right to eat. And so do I, because if I starve, Doreen starves.'

How do you think Mary feels when she realises her mum has cooked one of her racing pigeons? Support your answer with evidence from the text, referring back to the text to support your ideas.

[3 marks]

_____

_____

_____

_____

_____

_____

5

He struck a match. There was a candle on the table and he lighted it. By its thin little glimmer the children saw a large bare kitchen with a stone floor. There were no curtains, no **hearth-rug**. The chairs were in one corner and the pots, pans, brooms and crockery in another. There was no fire, and the black grate showed cold, dead ashes.

In the dining room there was a muddled maze of dusty furniture. There was a table certainly, and chairs, but there was no supper.

And in each room was the same kind of blundering half arrangement of furniture, but there was nothing to eat; even in the **pantry** there were only a rusty cake-tin and a broken plate.

Glossary

- **hearth-rug** rug on the floor in front of an open fire (the hearth) to protect the floor
- **pantry** cool storage cupboard for food and crockery

What does the text tell you about the last occupants of the house? Explain fully, using the text to support your answer. [3 marks]

_____

_____

_____

6

The tractor was ploughing faster and he was turning faster on the headlands too. Father was falling further and further behind all the time. There were nothing he could do about it. But he kept going and talking to the horses as he ploughed, sweetening them on like he always did. Go on then Joey. Giddyup. There's a boy. Good old girl Zoey. The crowd were on Father's side, most of them anyways. Everyone loves a loser I thought and there was tears coming in my eyes and I couldn't stop them neither. They were all clapping and whistling and cheering him every time he turned. So was I. But it didn't do Father nor the horses much good. I wanted to run off. I didn't ever want to look but I had to. I was there at the end of the furrow each time Father came back and he would give us a smile and I would try to give as good a one back. That weren't at all easy I can tell you.

What can you infer about how the narrator was feeling while his father was trying to plough as fast as the tractor? Explain fully, using the text to support your answer. [3 marks]

_____

_____

_____

! Top tips

- Find clues about characters, events or the plot that will help you answer the question.
- Put all the clues together and add them to the information you already know.
- Try to empathise with the central character(s). What would you do? How would you feel?
- Quote directly from the text, or paraphrase the text, to support your answer.
- Use the number of answer lines as guidance for how much you should write.

Explaining inferences in non-fiction

To achieve 100+ you need to use evidence from non-fiction texts to make **inferences** and **deductions**.

✔ What you need to know

- Writers often use clues to imply meaning or give a **biased** opinion in non-fiction texts.
- Good readers:
  - infer information that is not stated directly;
  - support their inferences with a precise explanation of the evidence.
- Inference requires a range of skills: asking questions, collecting and analysing evidence, making connections and predictions, making informed decisions and drawing conclusions.

★ Let's practise

> Some of our activities differed little from the days of peace. Our Troop meetings continued to be held in the Sunday School of the church for some months, but very quickly we became aware there was a war on. Immediately on the outbreak of war, the Government – fearing air raids on cities and large towns in industrial areas – ordered the evacuation of schoolchildren to places of safety. As a consequence, thousands of children of all ages came to Blackpool to live with, or as it was known, be billeted with, families.
>
> On arrival in Blackpool they went to schools to be taken to their billets; quite a number of Scouts went to the schools to act as messengers for three or four days. In retrospect, I am sure that as young lads living at home, we did not realise the anxiety of the evacuees, who had had to leave home without parents and live with people they had never met before!

Why do you think the Scouts did not understand how the evacuees felt?
Justify your answer with evidence from the text.

[3 marks]

1 Read the question and read it again. What is it asking?

The question is asking you to infer how the evacuees felt and to explain why the Scouts did not understand.

2	Find a fact relating to the evacuees.	They left their homes to live with other families in Blackpool.
3	What questions does this fact raise?	How did the evacuees feel? Might they have felt lonely, frightened and worried? They would have missed their families. I think that because that's how I might feel.
4	Would the Scouts have felt this?	No, because they were at home with their families.
5	Answer the question, making your point using inference, using the fact as your evidence and explaining it.	The Scouts would not understand how the evacuees felt because they had not been evacuated themselves. If you are evacuated, you leave your family and go to stay with another family in another place, *billeted with families*. If you have to leave your family as a child, you might feel frightened, worried and lonely. The Scouts would not feel this so would not understand the feelings of the children.
6	Check your answer.	

 **Try this**

1

> Volcanoes generate heat, known as geothermal energy. This renewable energy source can be harnessed, reducing reliance on non-renewable energy sources and benefiting the environment.
>
> The ash released during a volcanic eruption can benefit local agriculture by creating more fertile soils. This is because ash is a natural fertiliser which contains minerals that enhance the growth of crops. Areas with active volcanoes don't have to spend so much money on importing food to feed their population.
>
> Volcanoes are an important tourist attraction. Tourism benefits the local economy by creating jobs such as those in accommodation, transport, sightseeing and retail. Volcanoes can also discourage tourism. If the landscape is damaged by a volcanic eruption, or if tourists are put off by the fear of another eruption, the income of people living near volcanoes can be severely reduced.
>
> Volcanic eruptions are hazardous events. People can be killed by lava and poisonous gases. Property and livelihoods can also be damaged.
>
> Volcanic eruptions often lead to vital roads and other access routes being blocked, cutting areas off. Emergency services may have difficulty in reaching people and make recovering from volcanic disasters even harder.

Volcanic activity has both positive and negative effects.   *[3 marks]*
Explain fully what these effects are, referring to the text in your answer.

_____

_____

_____

2

Oh yes it is! Panto evolved from many different areas of entertainment and theatre. The most obvious is the stage play. Shakespeare is probably the best-known playwright in the world. In the days before telephone voting, the audience showed their displeasure by booing loudly or throwing rotten fruit. Far from sitting quietly in their seats, Shakespeare's audience played an active role in the drama.

It is essential to the show and is one reason for panto's lasting popularity. As far as 'Family Entertainment' goes, you can't do better than panto – for once, kids and parents are all on the same level, they're all 'in on the joke' and equally encouraged to sing along and shout out. All together now –

'Oh no they're not!'

'Oh yes they are!'

Why do you think audience participation has continued over the years?
Refer to the text in your answer.

[1 mark]

_____

_____

3

I went to St Matthias Primary on the Warwick Road in London. It was one of those old brick schools which look a bit like a prison or a hospital, with windows so high that you couldn't see out of them but just catch glimpses of blue sky.

I wasn't a very dazzling pupil and often made mistakes, which meant standing in the corner or being thwacked across the knuckles with a ruler. Books and stories became rather terrifying things, as the teacher was only interested in correct spelling and neat handwriting without any blotches. There was one good thing about school though, my first love, the brainy Belinda who I shared a desk with and whose work I tried to copy.

How would you describe the writer's memories of school?
Give evidence from the text to support your answer.

[3 marks]

_____

_____

_____

_____

4

> Shakespeare lived at a time when ordinary people didn't choose who ruled over them. Countries were ruled by someone who claimed that he (or, very rarely, she) had a right to rule because they belonged to a particular family. The people in this family would say there was a 'royal line' that went back and back which proved that they were the 'true' rulers. Many ordinary people looked up to these monarchs as if they were almost gods.
>
> Shakespeare wrote plays about the powerful families – the lords and dukes and princes – who wanted to rule England. In these plays, and in others set in Ancient Rome, we watch exciting scenes of civil wars, battles, rebellions, poor people's riots, conspiracies and wars between countries. And while all this is going on, the characters often discuss what makes a good ruler.

Explain fully why many of Shakespeare's plays included powerful characters who wanted to rule England.

Refer to the text in your answer.

[3 marks]

_____

_____

_____

5

> This ride will take you on a stomach-churning aerial adventure turning your world upside down at a height of up to eight metres. Take your seat and prepare for take-off, gliding from side to side at increasing heights whilst circling around the control tower. Before long, a series of gravity-defying barrel rolls in both directions will have you soaring and diving through the air. With banks, loops, dives and weightlessness to test even the most experienced riders, it promises to be the flight of your life.

What kind of people might enjoy this ride?
Explain using evidence from the text.

[1 mark]

_____

_____

_____

Top tips

- Use logic. Find examples that describe what is happening, where, when and how.
- Use your own knowledge and experience if possible, but make sure the text supports your answer.
- In question responses, you may need to refer to several pieces of evidence to show how they contribute to the overall meaning.

Explaining inferences in poetry

To achieve 100+ you need to make **inferences** and **deductions** in a range of poetry. This means identifying and explaining the ideas in a poem that may not actually be stated.

✓ What you need to know

- Poets try to say a lot with only a few words, so making inferences in poetry can be challenging.
- Poets sometimes deliberately keep you guessing about something that is not evident in the poem.
- Poets make effective use of language to encourage readers to use their imagination.
- There may be several pieces of evidence throughout the poem which, when combined together, show implied meaning.

★ Let's practise

Take the whisper of the river,
The thunder of the sea,
The echo of the songbird,
The rustle of the tree,
The howling of the blizzard,
The purring of the cat,
The shudder of the earthquake,
The whistle of the gnat,

The rumble of the stormcloud,
The singing of the sun,
The music of the moonrise,
And mix them one by one,
Till all the notes are silver
And all the chords are gold,
Then give your gift of laughter
To the sick, the sad, the old.

What might the title of this poem be? Explain using evidence from the text.

[1 mark]

1 Read the question and read it again. What is it asking?

The question is asking you to think of a suitable title for the poem and explain your choice.

2 Are there any clues in the structure of the poem? Look at the first word.

It begins with a command, *Take*, and is followed by a list.

3 Which writing genre do you know that uses commands and lists?

Instructions such as recipes, game rules, how to make things, spells.

30

4 Read on to find other clues to support this idea.

And mix them one by one . . . Then give your gift of laughter . . .

5 What is the main idea of the poem?

Mixing ingredients to make someone laugh.

6 Think of a suitable title to support the main idea and the writing genre you think it could be.

The title could be 'A recipe for happiness' because it tells the reader the ingredients, to *mix them one by one* and then to pass on this *gift of laughter* to others.

7 Check your answer.

Try this

1

This creature is elusive,	Scientists measure it
It slips by you	In light years,
In the blink of an eye.	Athletes in fractions of seconds.
Its tracks stretch endlessly	Watch out!
Backwards into the past,	There it goes!
And eternally forward into the future.	

What do you think the creature in the poem could be?   [1 mark]
Explain fully using the text to support your answer.

_____

_____

_____

2

It feels as if pins	I want to run away.
Are pricking my eyes,	But my legs are rooted to the ground
My face is burning hot.	Like trees. I have to stay
A firework is trying	And listen
To go off inside me.	To everyone calling me names
My feet are glued to the spot.	And not letting me
My hands are rocks in my pockets.	Join in with their games.

How do you think the narrator of the poem feels?   [2 marks]
Give **two** pieces of evidence to support your answer.

_____

_____

31

3

> **WANTED**:
> Knight in shining armour. V. pretty, but not so v. pretty in the morning.
> **Age (hers)**: N.O.Y.B.
> **Hobbies include**: Wound dressing, cooking meals and throwing in bin, biscuit eating (to Olympic level), asking 'Do I look fat to you?', building castles (sand only).
> **Seeking**: Non-squeamish male who can plan Civil War battles, write convincing sick notes and revive hamsters and goldfish.
> **Would prefer**: Professional footballer willing to spoil ungrateful and unruly children.
> **Would settle for**: Someone to make Mum laugh like drain or ticklish princess.

Do you think this poem is written from the perspective of the child or the mum? Use an example from the text to support your answer.

[1 mark]

_____

_____

_____

_____

4

> Live on cola, crisps and cake.
> Trade the gerbil for a snake.
> Fall asleep in front of the telly.
> Only wash when I'm really smelly.
> Leave my clothes all scattered about.
> Play loud music, scream and shout.
> Do what I feel like with my hair.
> Throw tantrums. Belch loud. Swear.
> Paint my bedroom red and black.
> Leave the dishes in a stack.
> Find out what it's like to be me.
> Let this list grow long… Get free!
> PS Take my savings in my hand.
> Buy a ticket to Laserland.

Who do you think the writer of the poem is?
Give **two** details to support your answer.

[2 marks]

_____

_____

> **! Top tips**
>
> - Look for clues in the structure of the poem (e.g. rhyming poem, conversational poem, nonsense poem).
> - Think about the theme, settings and characters of the poem.

5

A trick that everyone **abhors**
In little girls is slamming doors.
A wealthy banker's little daughter
Who lived in Palace Green, Bayswater
(By name Rebecca Offendort),
Was given to this furious sport.

She would deliberately go
And slam the door like billy-o!
To make her uncle Jacob start.
She was not really bad at heart,
But only rather rude and wild;
She was an aggravating child ...

It happened that a marble **bust**
Of Abraham was standing just
Above the door this little lamb
Had carefully prepared to slam,
And down it came! It knocked her flat!
It laid her out! She looked like that.

Her funeral sermon (which was long
And followed by a sacred song)
Mentioned her **virtues**, it is true,
But dwelt upon her **vices** too,
And showed the dreadful end of one
Who goes and slams the door for fun.

The children who were brought to hear
The awful tale from far and near
Were much impressed, and **inly** swore
They never more would slam the door,
– As often they had done before.

Glossary

- **abhors** hates
- **bust** a sculpture of a person's head, shoulders and chest
- **virtues** good standards of behaviour
- **vices** immoral or bad behaviour
- **inly** inwardly

Do you think Rebecca was a bad child?   [2 marks]
Support your answer with **two** examples from the text.

_____

_____

_____

Top tips

- Identify specific language used such as historical, scientific, words related to family, friends, etc.
- Identify features of language such as similes and metaphors that will give you clues to the meaning.

Making developed predictions

To achieve 100+ you need to predict what might happen next using evidence from the text.

✓ What you need to know

- Sometimes information in a text is stated outright and sometimes it is only implied.
- Good readers use clues in the text to explain what might happen next.
- **Prediction** questions are usually based on fiction texts.
- Your answers should refer to the plot, characters or events that have happened.
- Your answers should be written with detail, in one or two sentences, supported by evidence from the text.

Let's practise

"What is this place?" she asked.

"One o' th' kitchen-gardens," he answered.

"What is that?" said Mary, pointing through the other green door.

"Another of 'em," shortly.

"There's another on t'other side o' th' wall an' there's th' orchard t'other side o' that."

"Can I go in them?" asked Mary.

"If tha' likes. But there's nowt to see." Mary made no response. She went down the path and through the second green door. There she found more walls and winter vegetables and glass frames, but in the second wall there was another green door and it was not open. Perhaps it led into the garden which no one had seen for ten years. As she was not at all a timid child and always did what she wanted to do, Mary went to the green door.

> Based on what you have read, what might Mary do next?
> Use evidence from the text to support your prediction.

[2 marks]

1 Read the question and read it again. What is it asking?

The question is asking you to predict what Mary might do next.

2 Look at the text and find what Mary is doing in the extract.

She is exploring what is behind the doors in the garden. She wants to go through the green doors because she asks at the beginning *Can I go in them?*

3 Keep reading and find what Mary is doing at the end of the extract.

Mary finds another green door which is closed.

4 Look again at the passage for clues about Mary's character.

It says that she was not timid and that she always did what she wanted to do.

5 Link the evidence and clues together to predict what might happen next.

Mary will open the closed green door because she is brave and wants to know what is behind it.

6 Check your answer.

Try this

1

> A long time ago there lived a king who was famed for his wisdom through all the land. Nothing was hidden from him, and it seemed as if news of the most secret things was brought to him through the air. But he had a strange custom; every day after dinner, when the table was cleared, and no one else was present, a trusty servant had to bring him one more dish. It was covered, however, and even the servant did not know what was in it, neither did anyone know, for the king never took off the cover to eat of it until he was quite alone.
>
> This had gone on for a long time, when one day the servant, who took away the dish, was overcome with such curiosity that he could not help carrying the dish into his room. He knew that whatever the king was eating gave him these incredible powers and he wanted these powers as well. When he had carefully locked the door, he lifted up the cover, and saw a white snake lying on the dish.

Based on what you have read, what might the servant do next?   [2 marks]
Use evidence from the text to support your prediction.

_____

_____

_____

2

> Once upon a time there was a poor man named Gabriel. He lived in a little village with his wife. Over the hillside lived a very rich woman named Irene who claimed to be a princess cast out from her kingdom. She kept all her riches to herself and sneered at Gabriel, who could not even buy enough food to feed his wife.
>
> One day, Gabriel was walking through the village and happened to see a black hen tied up outside the weaver's hut. He walked on, thinking nothing of it. Later that day, a hysterical Irene ran over the hill exclaiming that her prize black hen had been stolen and crying for help. Gabriel in that instant realised that this was his opportunity to make his life better.

Explain using evidence from the text what Gabriel might do next. [2 marks]

_____

_____

_____

3

> A new study has suggested that around the year 2030 the Earth will enter a new wave of weather patterns. The Earth is only 15 years away from a period of low solar activity. Sunshine is predicted to fall by 60% creating conditions similar to the 17th century. During this time the cooling was so great that there was a mini ice age. The river Thames froze over and 'frost fairs' were held along the frozen river when Londoners could walk along it. The study claims it is extremely accurate and says that this phenomenon will occur when different fluid movements from the Sun converge together.

Use evidence from the article to explain what might happen to the Earth in 2030. [2 marks]

_____

_____

_____

! Top tips

- There will be clues in the text. Go back and look for them.
- Identify how characters behave, or how events unfold.
- Do not make up information or clues and do not answer with information that is not relevant to the text.
- Refer to key elements of plot, character or information in your answer.

4

Nicholas slipped back into the house and rapidly put into execution a plan of action that had long germinated in his brain. By standing on a chair in the library one could reach a shelf on which **reposed** a fat, important-looking key. The key was as important as it looked; it was the instrument which kept the mysteries of the **lumber-room** secure from unauthorised instruction, which opened a way for only aunts and such-like privileged persons. Nicholas had not had much experience of the art of fitting keys into keyholes and turning locks, but for some days past he had practised with the key of the schoolroom door; he did not believe in trusting too much to luck and accident.

Glossary
- **reposed** rested / sat
- **lumber-room** store room

Based on what you have read, what might Nicholas do next? [2 marks]
Use evidence from the text to support your prediction.

_____

_____

_____

5

1 Off to the beach
   Billy squashed in the car
   Promise of sea and sand
   Buckets and spades
   Sandwiches and lemonade
   Are we there yet?

2 There's the sea
   We all pile out
   Billy afloat
   Surfing swimming
   Digging dog chasing waves
   Oh what fun we had

3 Castle building
   Football playing
   Ice cream dripping
   Back in the surf
   Pony rides fun fair
   Oh what fun we had

4 Sun hidden warmth gone
   Time to go
   Back in the car
   Oh so far
   Mood had changed
   Are we there yet?

Explain using evidence from the poem how Billy's mood might have changed on the return journey. [2 marks]

_____

_____

_____

Understanding more about non-fiction

To achieve 100+ you need to find and explain how information is linked and contributes to the meaning of the whole text.

✓ What you need to know

- Every piece of information given contributes to the meaning of the whole text.
- The meaning of the text is what it is telling you.
- All the texts in this chapter are non-fiction.

★ Let's practise

Dragons are often believed to have major spiritual significance. In many Asian cultures dragons were **revered** as representative of the primal forces of nature, religion and the universe. They are associated with wisdom – often said to be wiser than humans – and longevity. They are commonly said to possess some form of magic or other supernatural power and are often associated with wells, rain and rivers. In some cultures, they are also said to be capable of human speech and in some traditions dragons are said to have taught humans to talk.

🔍 Glossary

- **revered** respected

Give **two** reasons why dragons are revered in some cultures.

[2 marks]

1	Read the question and read it again. What is it asking?	The question is asking why dragons are revered in some cultures. *Revered* is in the glossary: it means respected. So the question is asking why dragons are respected.
2	Read the text and find some reasons why dragons are respected.	It says they are associated with wisdom and thought to be wiser than humans, which would make them respected.
3	Keep reading. The question asks for two reasons.	They are said to possess some form of magic or supernatural power, which would make them powerful and respected.
4	Write your answer using both reasons.	Dragons are respected in some cultures because they are thought to be wiser than humans and possess magical powers.
5	Check your answer.	

Try this

1

Pizza, or one of its forms, has been a basic part of the Mediterranean diet since the Stone Age. This earliest form of pizza was crude bread that was baked beneath the stones of the fire. After cooking, it was seasoned with a variety of different toppings and was believed to have been used instead of plates and utensils to mop up broth or gravies. Some say that the idea of using bread as a plate came from the Greeks who ate flat round bread baked with an assortment of toppings. It was eaten by the working man and his family because it was a **thrifty** and convenient food. In the sixth century BC, at the height of the Persian Empire, it is said that the soldiers of Darius the Great, accustomed to lengthy marches, baked a kind of bread flat upon their shields and then covered it with cheese and dates.

Although you'd find many types of pitta or pizzas around the Mediterranean, it is in Naples that pizza in the form we know it today first emerged, after the tomato appeared on the table in the 1700s.

Glossary
- **thrifty** cheap

Explain why pizza was so popular in the past.

[1 mark]

_____

_____

2

Harthover had been built at 90 different times and in 90 different styles and looked as if somebody had built a whole street of houses of every imaginable shape and then stirred them together with a spoon.

For the attics were Anglo-Saxon. The third floor Norman. The second, **Cinquecento**. The first floor, Elizabethan. The right wing, Pure Doric. The centre, Early English, with a huge portico copied from the Parthenon. The left wing, pure **Boeotian**, which the country folk admired most of all because it was just like the new barracks in the town, only three times as big. The grand staircase was copied from the Catacombs at Rome. The back staircase from the Taj Mahal at Agra. The cellars were copied from the caves of Elephanta. The offices from the Pavilion at Brighton.

Glossary
- **Cinquecento** from the 1500s
- **Boeotian** from a region of Greece called Boeotia

Use evidence from the text to explain the line Harthover *looked as if somebody had ... stirred them together with a spoon.*

[2 marks]

_____

_____

3

The Eden Project is an exciting attraction where you can explore your relationship with nature, learn new things and get inspiration from the world around you.

Top 10 reasons to visit the Eden Project

Here's some of what you'll find when you visit:

- The world's largest rainforest in captivity with steamy jungles and waterfalls.

- Cutting-edge architecture and buildings.

- Stunning garden displays all year round.

- World-class sculpture and art.

- Evening gigs, concerts and an ice rink in the winter.

- Educational centre and demonstrations to inspire all ages.

- Brilliant local, fairly traded food in the restaurants and cafés.

- A rainforest canopy walkway, where you can take a stunning walk among the treetops.

- Living example of regeneration and **sustainable** living.

- Free ride on our land train, often pulled by a tractor.

Glossary

- **sustainable** using resources carefully

What is meant by the sentence *you can explore your relationship with nature*?

Give evidence from the text to explain how you can do this at the Eden Project.

[2 marks]

_____

_____

_____

_____

Top tips

- Remember to use the glossary for words in bold.
- Remember to answer both parts of the question.
- Explain in your own words; do not just copy sentences from the text.
- When you are asked for evidence, find things that are in the text. You can copy these.
- Make sure your evidence relates to the point you are making.

4

In 1966, a farmer in Tully, Australia, allegedly spotted what he called a 'flying saucer' rising up from a swampy area of land. When he went to investigate the site, he came across a flattened circular area of grassland that he assumed had been caused by the saucer.

This is claimed to be the first spotting of a crop circle and sparked further reports of sightings over the decades, many in England, peaking particularly in the 1980s and 1990s, gaining mass-media attention.

In 1991, two men named Bower and Chorley confessed to being the creators of dozens of crop circles across the UK, saying they wanted the public to believe that aliens were responsible.

Since this confession, crop circles have generally made headlines for their incredible sizes, designs and complexity and it is assumed they are the work of human artists, not extraterrestrial ones.

Underline **two** phrases that show many people were interested in these crop circles.

[2 marks]

5

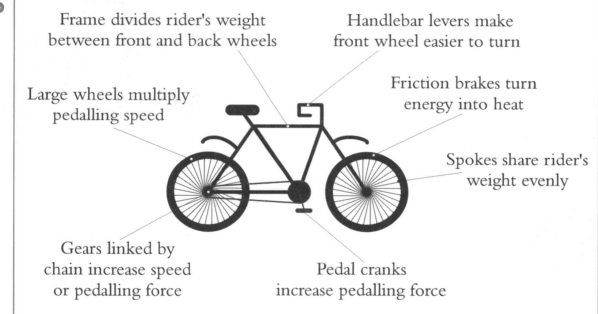

Frame divides rider's weight between front and back wheels

Handlebar levers make front wheel easier to turn

Large wheels multiply pedalling speed

Friction brakes turn energy into heat

Spokes share rider's weight evenly

Gears linked by chain increase speed or pedalling force

Pedal cranks increase pedalling force

Underline **two** different words that might persuade a reader that this bicycle is a good purchase.

[1 mark]

Top tips

- Read the question carefully and check how many words or phrases it is asking you to underline.
- When it asks for only one word do not underline any other words.
- Use a ruler when underlining.

Understanding more about fiction

To achieve 100+ you need to find and explain how events are linked and contribute to the meaning of the whole text.

 What you need to know

- Everything that happens in a story contributes to the meaning of the whole text.
- The meaning of the text is what it is telling you.
- All the texts in this chapter are fiction.

Let's practise

When you are young life leaves you no choice
Do this. Do that.
No room for a little voice
When all you want to do is play and just have fun
Ride your bike, roller-skate, and be free to run.
With no concerns for the who's, what's, when's and why's
Then you go from a girl to a woman before your own eyes.
Life gives you lessons to learn as you grow
Room for mistakes and time to show what you know
Just be patient because things will soon go your way
enjoy the young times and have a happy birthday!

Explain why the poem shifts from talking about a girl to a woman.

[1 mark]

1	Read the question and read it again. What is it asking?	The question is asking you to explain why it starts talking about a girl and then goes on to talk about a woman.
2	Read the text and find where it changes.	It is in the middle where it says *Then you go from a girl to a woman before your own eyes*. This suggests she is growing up.
3	Carry on reading and find why you think it is suggesting she is growing up.	The poem finishes *have a happy birthday*. You grow older on your birthday so that must be why.
4	Write your answer. Then, check your answer.	The girl in the poem is growing older because it is her birthday.

Try this

1

One day a fox came upon a grape orchard and found a
bunch of beautiful grapes hanging from a high branch.
'Those grapes would be really tasty,' he thought to himself.
The fox prepared to reach up to the grapes by running
from a distance and jumping as high as he could, but he
did not jump high enough. The fox tried again and he
almost got high enough but he still could not reach the
grapes. He tried again and again, but he just couldn't jump
high enough to reach the grapes. Finally, he gave up and as
he walked away, he put his nose in the air and said, 'I am
sure those grapes are sour anyway.'

Explain how the fox's attitude towards the grapes changed at the end of
the extract.

[1 mark]

_____

_____

2

Even though they were sisters, Suzie and June were nothing alike. If Suzie wanted
to play netball, June wanted to draw. If June wanted to watch soap operas, Suzie
wanted to watch cartoons. Tensions rose to the point that the girls could no longer
stand one another's company. It seemed that they had nothing in common, until
the day that progress reports came out. The girls realised that they were both
struggling in one subject at school. Suzie was struggling in maths and June was
struggling in reading. Since both girls wanted to do their best at school, they
agreed to help each other. Every day after school for the next few weeks, Suzie
helped June with reading and June helped Suzie in maths. By the time reports were
handed out, Suzie and June were excelling in all subjects. The girls were delighted,
but their parents were happiest of all. Not just because their daughters passed
their classes, but because they had learned to be good sisters.

Explain how the girls learned to be good sisters.

[1 mark]

_____

_____

Top tips

- Remember to explain in your own words.
- Do not just copy sentences from the text.

3

Billy doesn't like school really,
It's not because he can't do the work
but because some of the other kids
don't seem to like him that much.

They call him names
and make up jokes about his mum.

Everyone laughs… except Billy.
Everyone laughs… except Billy.

They all think it's OK
because it's only a laugh and a joke
and they don't really mean it anyway
but Billy doesn't know that.

Billy doesn't know that
and because of that
Billy doesn't like school really.

Explain why *everyone laughs… except Billy* in the poem.

[1 mark]

_____

_____

4

Florrie crouched down low behind the crumbling, marble headstone. The night was pitch black, broken only by the occasional glimmer of the haunting moon from behind dense clouds.

She shivered as the wind caught the **arthritic** branches, reaching out to touch the icy emptiness of the air. It would only be a matter of minutes until she could come out of hiding, only a matter of minutes until she would be safe. Florrie rubbed her hands together for warmth, and as she did so, she could feel the dull pounding of her rhythmic heart. 'Be quiet,' she whispered, knowing there would be no answer. Florrie felt as if she was being watched. Should she stay or should she run? What was that towering over her? She just didn't dare to turn round. It could be her worst nightmare come true. 'Don't panic, don't panic,' she repeated over and again in her head.

Glossary
• **arthritic** old and creaky

Underline **two** phrases that tell us that Florrie is scared.

[2 marks]

5

When young Jenny Philips accidentally discovers a glowing suitcase in her attic, she is swiftly teleported to a new world, many centuries into the future, to planet Melton. Captured and ordered to work at the space research station, Jenny is given the mission to create a vehicle which can teleport the Meltons back to her world. Jenny knows little about physics, but teams up with a tiny Melton named Pluton, who helps her to understand more about the theory of relativity and the speed of light. But Jenny soon discovers that the intentions of the Meltons aren't purely welcoming. She learns that their plan is to continue their lifelong study of human thinking, which involves looking closely at the structure of the human brain. With Pluton's help, Jenny attempts to create a time-travelling vehicle that will leave the Meltons in no doubt that no one messes with humans on planet Earth!

Find and **copy one** phrase where Jenny finds that the Meltons are not quite as kind as she initially thought.

[1 mark]

_____

_____

! Top tips

- Read the question carefully and check how many words or phrases it is asking you copy or to underline.
- When it asks for a phrase copy or underline the group of words that fit the answer best.
- You do not need to copy or underline a whole sentence, just a phrase.
- Remember to reread the question afterwards to check whether it is asking you for two phrases.
- Use a ruler when underlining.

Discussing language choices in fiction

To achieve 100+ you need to identify and explain how a writer's choice of language enhances meaning in a fiction text.

✔ What you need to know

- Writers use language in different ways to keep readers interested. For example, they use **imagery** to produce vivid images in readers' minds and to encourage readers to connect with texts, to increase enjoyment and develop thinking skills.
- One way to create imagery is to use **figurative language**. This is language that has a different meaning from the literal or 'usual' meaning. Examples include **simile**, **metaphor**, **alliteration**, **onomatopoeia** and **personification**.
- Writers also create imagery by using **idioms**. These are phrases that mean something different to how they sound. For example, writing *raining cats and dogs* instead of *pouring down* and writing *a piece of cake* instead of *something that can be accomplished easily*.

★ Let's practise

Gulliver felt a tickle of movement on his legs and body, and, before long, the little archer was joined by a dozen more like him.

'I must be going mad …' Gulliver murmured at last. Then he yelled, 'Get off me!' and the archers screamed and ran for their lives.

Gulliver strained against his bonds and managed to free his arms. He instantly heard a soft whooshing noise and realised that the little archers were shooting at him. Their tiny arrows prickled into his hands and face like a host of wasp stings, several only just missing his eyes. The pain told him he wasn't mad, and that what was happening was all too real!

a) What does the writer compare the arrows to? [1 mark]

b) Explain the effect of the comparison. [1 mark]

1 Read the question and read it again. What is it asking?

The question is asking you to identify what the arrows are being compared to and explain the effect of this comparison.

2 Find what the arrows are being compared to and identify the language feature.

like a host of wasp stings is a simile comparing the pricking of the arrows to wasp stings.

3 What effect does the simile have on the reader?

It uses the reader's experience of wasp stings to give an understanding of the pain Gulliver felt each time an arrow pricked him.

4 Check your answer.

 *Try this*

1

> We had until then to get as far away as possible. Big Black Jack didn't want to trot for long, but he plodded on steadily, never tiring, and we sat up there the two of us, rocking our way towards the grey light of dawn.
>
> We were just so happy to be out of Cooper's Station. We talked a lot as we rode, and we laughed, laughed as hard as we could. I remember I felt cocooned by the night, swallowed up in its immensity, protected.

Why is the phrase *I felt cocooned by the night* an effective phrase to describe how the narrator feels? Explain your answer fully, referring to the text.   [2 marks]

_____

_____

2

> As they entered the theme park, Harry and Dad discovered a height gauge. Harry's face dropped.
>
> The sign next to the gauge read, 'Riders must be 1m 50cm or over to ride the roller coaster'. Harry knew that he wasn't as tall as the other boys in his class. Undoubtedly, he wouldn't be tall enough now!
>
> Reluctantly, Harry stood against the measuring stick. He didn't really want to know what it said. He didn't really want to be measured. What he really wanted to do was to ride the roller coaster. That's all!
>
> He considered the expression on Dad's face …

a) **Find** and **copy** the phrase that tells you Harry wasn't happy.   [1 mark]

_____

_____

b) Explain the effect of using this phrase.   [1 mark]

_____

_____

_____

3

The crew wrestled the lifeboat into the sea, and they all jumped into it. They rowed away, hoping to find land. But the sea had other plans, and before long, a giant wave swamped them. Robinson fell into the foaming sea and felt himself being sucked down. He held his breath till he thought his lungs would burst. Then he was driven back to the surface, and the sea dumped him on a beach, the waves hissing and bubbling as they retreated.

Three times the terrible sea caught him, even though he tried his best to outrun it, and three times it swallowed him and spat him out, but always further and further up the beach. At last it left him alone, and he crawled painfully into the shelter of some palm trees.

a) What is the writer comparing the sea to?   [1 mark]

     Tick ✔one.

the waves   ☐

the water   ☐

an animal   ☐

a plant   ☐

b) Explain the effect of using this comparison using **two** examples from the text.   [2 marks]

_____

_____

4

As a schoolboy in Ancient Greece you were supposed to learn reading, writing and music but, most importantly, you had to be brave. Teachers toughened up their pupils by hitting them whenever they stepped out of line. In fact, the word for 'teach' in Greek is the same as the word for 'whack with a big stick'.

Teachers toughened up their pupils by hitting them whenever they stepped out of line.   [1 mark]

Explain what the phrase *stepped out of line* tells you about the children's experience of school in Ancient Greece.

_____

_____

_____

5

> Every Spartan boy had one aim: to be the best soldier around. Seven-year-old boys were sent away from home to start training. They weren't taught to read and write, just to be as tough as possible. They weren't given enough food or warm clothes, even in winter. They slept on itchy straw until they were 14 and after that on rushes which were even spikier.
>
> Yes, Spartans definitely did things differently. Spartan kids were actually encouraged to steal stuff. The idea was that when they grew up and fought wars in foreign countries they'd be able to nick themselves some dinner. No one minded if you stole something – but there was hell to pay if you got caught.

a) **Find** and **copy** the phrase that suggests the consequences would be severe for boys who were not very good at stealing. [1 mark]

_____

_____

b) What effect does the phrase have on the reader? [1 mark]

_____

_____

6

> The green of the garden was greyed over with dew; indeed, all its colours were gone until the touch of sunrise. The air was still, and the tree-shapes crouched down upon themselves. One bird spoke; and there was a movement when an awkward parcel of feathers dislodged itself from the tall fir-tree at the corner of the lawn, seemed for a second to fall and then at once swept up and along, outspread, on a wind that never blew, to another, farther tree: an owl. It wore the ruffled, dazed appearance of one who has been up all night.

a) **Find** and **copy one** example of personification. [1 mark]

_____

b) Explain its effect. [1 mark]

_____

! Top tips

- Name the language feature in your answer.
- Use clues from the text to justify your answer.
- Describe how the language feature builds a better picture or changes the emotions of the reader.
- Look to see how many lines are provided for the answer. More lines mean you could achieve additional marks by providing more detail in your answer.

Discussing language choices in poetry

To achieve 100+ you need to explain how a writer's choice of words, phrases and language features enhance meaning in poetry.

✓ What you need to know

- Poets try to engage with the reader's feelings by using humour, sorrow, adoration and jealousy as well as many other emotions.
- Poets use language in a creative way to produce vivid images and to encourage readers to connect with poems, to increase enjoyment and develop thinking skills.
- One way poets create images is to use figurative language. This is language whose meaning is different from the literal or 'usual' meaning. Examples include simile, metaphor, alliteration, onomatopoeia and personification.
- Poets also use language to give rhythm and flow to words, to add rhymes and repetition of words and sounds. These features affect how the poem sounds when you read it. They can also help to communicate the poem's meaning and can impact on the reader.

★ Let's practise

The wind was a torrent of darkness among the gusty trees,
The moon was a ghostly galleon tossed upon cloudy seas,
The road was a ribbon of moonlight over the purple moor,
And the highwayman came riding –
    Riding – riding –
The highwayman came riding, up to the old inn-door.

a) What language feature does the writer use to describe the setting? *[1 mark]*

b) Explain the effect of this, referring to the poem in your answer. *[1 mark]*

1 Read the question and read it again. What is it asking?

The question is asking you to identify a language feature and say how it adds to the meaning of the text.

50

2 Look at how the setting is described.

It says that the wind, the moon and the road are all something else.

3 Which language feature does this?

metaphor

4 How do the metaphors build a better picture of the setting?

They compare each thing to something else. Each sentence continues with a phrase giving further description.

5 Give an example to explain what you mean.

The poem compares the moon to a ghostly galleon. It then describes how the moon would move through the clouds like a galleon through the sea.

6 How does the description help the reader imagine the scene? What is its effect?

The poem uses metaphors to describe aspects of the setting as other objects. The descriptions of their images and actions build up a better picture of the night setting. For example, the moon is described as a ghostly galleon moving through the clouds.

7 Check your answer.

Try this

1

Faster than fairies, faster than witches,
Bridges and houses, hedges and ditches;
And charging along like troops in a battle
All through the meadows the horses and cattle:
All of the sights of the hill and the plain
Fly as thick as driving rain;
And ever again, in the wink of an eye,
Painted stations whistle by.

In this poem about a train, what effect does the writer want to create by using the words *faster*, *charging*, *fly* and *whistle by*?

[1 mark]

_____

_____

2

Fillet of a fenny snake,
In the cauldron boil and bake;
Eye of newt, and toe of frog,
Wool of bat and tongue of dog,
Adder's fork, and blind worm's sting,
Lizard's leg, and owlet's wing,
For a charm of powerful trouble,
Like a hell broth boil and bubble.
Double, double, toil and trouble:
Fire, burn; and cauldron, bubble.

What emotion does the writer want the reader to feel when reading this poem?

Explain fully, referring to the text in your answer.

[1 mark]

_____

_____

_____

_____

3

'I can can-can
Can you can-can?'
'Yes, I can can-can, too.
In fact, I can can-can
Very, very well.
I can can-can better than you.'
'No, you can't can-can
better than I can can-can
because I can can-can better!'
'Bet you can't!'
'Bet I can!'
'Bet you can't!'
'Bet I can! I can! I can can-can better!'

What is the effect of repeating the word *can* throughout this poem?

Refer to the text in your answer.

[1 mark]

_____

_____

_____

_____

4

Ernie watched so much TV
He put down roots in the settee,
At night he never went to bed,
He vegetated there instead.

He stared and stared, hour after hour,
His face became a pale white flower.
Green leaves sprouted from his hair.
He drove his parents to despair.

His mother fetched a watering can,
'You'll never grow into a man,'
She sighed and, sprinkling him with care,
She pulled some weeds out of his hair.

Explain how the writer uses language to describe Ernie.
Refer to the text in your answer.

[*1 mark*]

_____

_____

_____

_____

Top tips

- Identify the language feature being used and name it in your answer, if this is relevant.
- If the feature is a comparative one, say which things are being compared.
- Explain how the language feature builds a better image for the reader by giving an example from the text of a sound, a size, a movement, etc.

Making comparisons

To achieve 100+ you need to make **comparisons** in a text.

 What you need to know

- It is important to compare information, characters or events in the text.
- The text will be non-fiction.
- When giving your answer, quote directly from the text, using inverted commas, or paraphrase (use your own words).

Let's practise

In 1539, the first modern Christmas tree was erected in the cathedral at Strasbourg, Germany. Christmas trees became part of the British Christmas after Prince Albert and Queen Victoria married in 1840.

In Victorian Britain, the first Christmas trees were decorated with candles, sweets, fruit and home-made decorations. Whereas, according to German tradition, the first trees were decorated only with edible decorations such as nuts, gingerbread and apples.

[1 mark]

What is different about the decoration of Victorian Christmas trees compared to the first German trees?

1	Read the question and read it again. What is it asking?	The question is asking you to compare the decorations of two types of tree.
2	Look for a word which compares the two tree decorations.	*Whereas*
3	What were Victorian trees decorated with?	edible decorations, candles and home-made decorations
4	What were German trees decorated with?	edible decorations

5 Which decorations are present on the Victorian tree that are missing on the German tree?

candles and home-made decorations

6 Answer the question referring to both trees, giving evidence from the text.

The difference is that though they were both decorated with edible foods, the German tree was not decorated with candles and home-made decorations like the Victorian tree.

7 Check your answer.

Try this

1

I was hot and dusty and thirsty on the bus, and I thought the journey would never end, but I was happy. I was happy to have arrived, happy not to be sea-sick any more. Tired though we were, we were buoyed up by the excitement of it all. This was a new adventure in a new world. We were on a bus ride into a wonderland and we were loving it, every single moment of it.

'Your new home,' the man told us, opening the door. I didn't take much notice of him, not then. I was too busy looking around me.

I think it was from the moment they first shut us in the **dormitory** block at Cooper's Station, and we heard the door bolted behind us, that I have hated walls about me and locked doors. I was about to find out, as we all were, not what it was *like* to be a prisoner but what it *was* to be a prisoner.

Glossary

- **dormitory** a large room containing a large number of beds

[2 marks]

How do the feelings of the writer change from the beginning of the text to the end?

_____

_____

_____

Top tips

- Words such as *like, unlike, but, even though, while, however, although, whereas, in common* indicate that the text is written to compare and contrast.
- Comparative adjectives may be used to make comparisons such as: *taller than, greater than, better / worse, more / less.*
- When possible, refer to both parts of the text you are comparing, to make your answer clearer.

2

Features	Animal cell	Plant cell
Cell wall	absent	present
Shape	round (irregular)	rectangular (fixed)
Chloroplasts	none	present to make their own food
Cytoplasm	present	present
Nucleus	present	present

Compare and contrast what you have read about animal cells and plant cells.

a) What are the similarities between them?   [1 mark]

_____

_____

b) What are the differences between them?   [1 mark]

_____

_____

3

One of the most common questions is, 'What is the difference between toads and frogs?'

Characteristics of frogs:
- two bulging eyes
- strong, long, webbed hind feet and legs are adapted for leaping and swimming
- smooth or slimy skin (generally, frogs tend to like more moist environments)
- frogs tend to lay eggs in clusters
- can be found all over the world on every continent except Antarctica

Characteristics of toads:
- poison glands behind the eyes
- toads tend to lay eggs in long chains
- can be found worldwide except in Australasia, polar regions, Madagascar and Polynesia
- stubby bodies with short hind legs (for walking instead of hopping)
- warty and dry skin (usually preferring drier climates)

a) Name **two** ways frogs and toads are different.   [2 marks]

_____

_____

b) Name **one** way frogs and toads are similar.   [1 mark]

_____

4

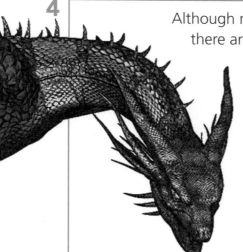

Although many dragons occur in legends from around the world, there are many differences in the dragons portrayed. While they are commonly portrayed as **serpentine** or reptilian, hatching from eggs and possessing typically scaly or feathered bodies, some dragons are said to breathe fire or to be poisonous, such as in the old English poem 'Beowulf'. European dragons are more often winged, while Chinese dragons resemble large snakes. Dragons may have a variable number of legs: none, two, four, or more when it comes to early European literature.

Glossary
- **serpentine** snake-like

a) What is different about European dragons compared to Chinese dragons? [1 mark]

_____

_____

b) What do most dragons have in common? Name **two** things. [2 marks]

1. _____

2. _____

5

They clattered into the hallway. Tom put the blacks up in the front room, crashed around in the darkness and lit the gas and oil lamps. After he had made a pot of tea they sat near the range and surveyed each other.

Willie's face, hair and clothes were covered in earth. His filthy hands showed up starkly against the white mug he was holding. Zach, Tom discovered, was a **voluble**, curly haired boy a few months older than Willie, only taller and in bad need, so he thought, of a haircut. A red jersey was draped around his bare shoulders and a pair of frayed, rather colourful, men's braces held up some well-darned green shorts.

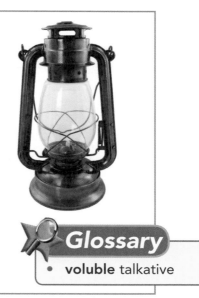

Glossary
- **voluble** talkative

Write **two** ways Zach is different to Willie. [2 marks]
Use evidence from the text to support your answer.

1. _____

2. _____

Glossary

Alliteration A series of words in which the same sound is repeated.

Biased Unfairly preferring one idea over another.

Compare To make a link between two similar things.

Context Background information to make the meaning clearer.

Deduction A conclusion reached using facts or reasoning.

Figurative language Phrases whose meaning is different from the usual meaning.

Idiom An expression that has a different meaning from the usual meaning of the words (e.g. *over the moon* means very happy).

Imagery Using words to allow the reader to paint images in their imagination.

Inference A conclusion reached on the basis of reasoning and evidence.

Key details Specific information that contributes to the main idea in a piece of writing.

Main idea The most important piece of information the writer wants you to know.

Metaphor When one object is described as another: *the sun is a golden apple*.

Onomatopoeia Language imitating the sound of an object or action.

Paraphrase To reword something written or spoken using different words.

Personification Language giving human qualities to an animal or object.

Prediction Working out what will happen next using the information you are given.

Quotation marks Punctuation used to mark the beginning and end of a quoted passage.

Retrieve To find something in a text (usually information).

Scan To search for specific information.

Simile A way to compare one thing to another using the words 'like' or 'as'.

Skim To read quickly to note the important points.

Summarise To give a brief statement of the main points.

Answers

Note: *Answers provided are suggestions. Always use professional judgement when considering children's responses.*

Explaining the meaning of words in context (pages 9–11)

1 To describe the height of the river.
   It tells you that the river is low. / To see a crocodile lying in it, the water would have to be low.

2 To create something means to make something. / They are made or created by people. / They have been made and are not natural.

3 It describes how the water is rotten by the smell which is stinking, foul-smelling and disgusting.

4 a) a problem for the environment
   b) The silicone doesn't break down naturally which is a problem and could add to landfill. It also is a risk to land and sea animals who swallow them. They could choke, get caught in them or become very ill.

5 It tells you that it was difficult to get the boat into the water because it was so rough. / It tells you that they struggled to get the boat into the rough sea. / It tells you that they had a tough fight on their hands to get the boat into the sea.

6 More than enough to eat. / Lots. / It says she brought 'plate after plate' with cake on them which tells you they had lots of food.

Retrieving information and identifying key details (pages 13–17)

1 a) heavily. b) an earthquake. c) Russia. d) huge.

2 a) generous. b) the 18th century. c) pudding ingredients. d) a kiss.

3 1 mark for all four correct: true, false, false, true

4 1 mark for all four correct: false, true, false, true

5 2 marks for all three correct. 1 mark for two correct answers.

Which two ports are the ships in the Santa Barbara Channel using?	Los Angeles and Long Beach
What is the danger whales face from the ships?	Serious injury/death
What are the shipping companies being asked to do in the test?	Slow their speed. / Slow down.

Summarising main ideas (pages 19–21)

1 Award 2 marks for any two of the following: This is not a good / close relationship. / Alexander is trying hard to please his father but there is nothing he can do. / His father is not impressed and says he was 'better when I was' Alexander's age. / His father told him when he was 'clumsy'. / His father made him nervous when he tried to impress him, and was 'quick to tell him' when he was clumsy.

2 1 mark for answers related to swimming as a form of exercise and / or leisure for all, for example: In the swim; Fun and Swimfit in the pool; Swim for your life; Everyone

dive in. 1 mark for explanation related to the choice of headline: The text describes the benefits of swimming, such as to stretch athletes and to pass time. / The text talks about the benefits of swimming as a cheap way to get fit or spend your time.

3 He was too busy thinking about his land that was ruled by the Viking warriors. / He was too caught up in reading his book that he forgot to look at the bread.

4 1 mark for a suitable subtitle: Natural medicines; Medicines; Cures from a rainforest; Natural and modern medicines working together; Modern medicines made from natural ingredients. 1 mark for an explanation: The text explains that many modern medicines are derived / based on / come from natural products.

5 How Halloween traditions have evolved or changed; Changing Halloween traditions; How Halloween has become the tradition it is today
   The text explains that traditions or things we do on Halloween have changed over the years and in different places.

6 Award 1 mark for the main idea that David wanted to be like a grown-up and fight the Philistines with his family. Award 1 mark for evidence from the text that shows that his father / brothers thought he was too young, e.g. David says he wants to face the Philistines but Jesse said he was not old enough.

Explaining inferences in fiction (pages 23–25)

1 Award 3 marks for fully developed answer with reference to the text:
   Mr Carter must have treated his Indian workers badly, like slaves. He was becoming poor because his workers had disappeared and had stopped working for him. It says, 'If you treat them like slaves they don't revolt or go on strike; they simply melt back into the forest, join their tribes and disappear.' This proves he treated them badly.
   Award 2 marks for developed answer with reference to the text:
   He treated the workers badly because they stopped working for him and went back into the forest.
   Award 1 mark for undeveloped points:
   He treated them badly. / He didn't pay them enough. / He didn't respect them.

2 That she would not let him stay off school because in the past when he'd invented diseases she had still made him go: '…he knew from experience that his mother would make him face school …'.
   If he really was sick, his mother would still make him go to school because in the past '… his mother always prescribed breakfast and a bracing walk to school as the cure'.

3 1 mark: a collector; an explorer; a naturalist; a scientist. 1 mark for evidence from the text: He collected plants. / He kept jars for his specimens. / He had a dissecting kit and a microscope.

4 Award 3 marks for fully developed response with reference to the text:
   Mary is angry with her mum because it says 'Mary's

voice rose'. This means that she started speaking loudly, which is a sign of anger. it also says that Mary was 'infuriated' by her mum's logic. If you are infuriated you are very angry.

Award 2 marks for developed response with reference to the text:

Mary is really angry with her mum because she raised her voice.

Award 1 mark for undeveloped response: Mary was angry/furious/cross with her mum.

5 Award 3 marks for fully developed response with more than one reference to the text:

The occupants had left a long time ago and had left in a hurry. The furniture in the house is all over the place in a 'muddled maze' so they must have either piled it up or not bothered to put it in its right place and it was dusty./The fire had been out for a long time. It had 'cold, dead ashes' and there was no 'hearth-rug' which means it hadn't been lit in a long time./There was no food to eat and there was a rusty cake tin and a broken plate which means they hadn't eaten or prepared food for a long time either.

Award 2 marks for developed response with reference to the text:

They had left a long time ago and in a hurry because the furniture is all over the place and it was dusty.

The fire had been out for a long time and there was no 'hearth-rug'./

There was no food to eat and there was a rusty cake tin.

Award 1 mark for undeveloped points:

They left in a hurry./They left a long time ago.

6 Award 3 marks for fully developed response with reference to the text:

He felt quite upset and hurt that his father could not go as fast as the tractor. He had tears in his eyes and even though he was cheering it didn't do 'much good' which means it wasn't enough./He wanted to run off and he didn't want to look at his father falling behind which means that he was upset to see his father losing.

Award 2 marks for developed response with reference to the text:

He was upset that his father couldn't go as fast as the tractor. He didn't want to watch.

Award 1 mark for undeveloped points:

He was sad and upset for his dad.

Explaining inferences in non-fiction (pages 27–29)

1 Award 3 marks for a fully developed, text-based explanation for both positive and negative outcomes.
Award 2 marks for a fully developed, text-based explanation of either a positive or a negative outcome.
Award 1 mark for two undeveloped points.
Positive answers related to money, agriculture, tourism, renewable energy. Volcanoes can benefit an area through creating money and jobs through tourism or agriculture and can provide cheap energy. They provide food so money doesn't have to be spent on importing or buying food.
Negative answers related to suffering of local people, damage to environment, decrease in tourism. People could die due to lava flow and gases. They also cause

damage to people's lives and property – they could lose their homes and their livelihoods – so in the future or long term people's lifestyles and jobs might be at risk, especially if there is another eruption likely.

2 They have continued to join in because they enjoy/have always been allowed to be part of the action. In Shakespeare's time, the audience booed and threw fruit. In modern panto they sing along and call out.

3 Award 3 marks for fully developed response with reference to the text:

They weren't good memories. He did not like school because he was not bright and he didn't like books and stories. He describes the building like a prison./He made mistakes, was stood in the corner and hit with a ruler./He was terrified of books. These are bad memories and you wouldn't like school if you made mistakes and were hit.

Award 2 marks for developed response with reference to the text:

He had bad memories of school because bad things happened to him like being hit with a ruler and standing in the corner.

Award 1 mark for undeveloped points:

He had bad memories./He didn't like school./He remembered bad things that happened to him. Also accept 1 mark for a good memory of school because of his first love, 'the brainy Belinda'.

4 Award 3 marks for fully developed response with reference to the text:

He wanted to show the ordinary people what the powerful rulers of England were like at the time./The characters discussed what made a good ruler. This means that the ordinary people could see what he thought powerful families who wanted to rule did or how they behaved/acted./He wanted to show people what he thought made a good ruler because ordinary people might not know/understand/be able to see this.

Award 2 marks for developed response with reference to the text:

He wanted to show the ordinary people what the powerful rulers of England were like at the time because they might not know. The characters discussed what made a good ruler.

Award 1 mark for undeveloped points:

To show people what they were like./To show people what they did.

5 People who are brave/fearless/thrill seekers/daredevils/not frightened of speed or heights/like excitement.

You need to be someone who is not afraid of heights as you will be 'soaring and diving through the air'.

Explaining inferences in poetry (pages 31–33)

1 It could be time. Clues are that time can go quickly, in the blink of an eye, you can go back in time to the past and into the future. /Light years are measured in time./Seconds are used in measuring time.

2 Award 2 marks for identifying that the writer feels lonely, frightened, upset and angry and for including two pieces of evidence.

Lines 1, 2 and 3 suggest wanting to cry.

Lines 4 and 5 suggest anger.

Lines 6, 7, 8 and 9 suggest they are too scared to run away.

Lines 10–14 suggest they are being called names and they want to join in but no one will let them play.

3 I think it is written by the child.

When it gives details about the mum, they are not very nice implying she is not so pretty in the morning and she eats lots of biscuits.

A mum wouldn't write this about herself.

It describes all the things a child might want, such as someone to play with, to write sick notes, to play football with, to spoil children. These are things a child would write to get things for themselves.

4 Award 2 marks for answers related to children/teenagers who wish to be rebellious/disobedient/unruly.

Answer to include any two examples from the poem.

5 Award 2 marks for answers that include two suitable examples from the text, such as:

I do think she was really bad because she did things that hurt or annoyed others such as being rude, wild, aggravating, slamming doors to upset her uncle. At her funeral they talked about her vices which means she did other bad things too.

I don't think she was really bad because verse 2 says she 'was not really bad at heart', she was just 'rude and wild'.

I don't think she deliberately meant to drop the bust, it just fell when she slammed the door too hard. At her funeral, they mentioned her virtues, which means she wasn't always bad.

Making developed predictions (pages 35–37)

1 2 marks. Award 1 mark for predicting that the servant might eat the snake.

Award 1 mark for evidence: he knew that what the king was eating gave him these powers./He wanted the same powers that the king had.

2 2 marks. Award 1 mark for predicting that Gabriel might say he knows where her hen is to be found./Telling her where her hen is.

Award 1 mark for evidence that he will ask for money to make his life better./Irene is rich and Gabriel is poor.

3 2 marks. Award 1 mark for predicting that it will get colder/freeze.

Award 1 mark for evidence that sunshine is predicted to reduce./Last time this happened there was a mini ice age./The study claims to be accurate.

4 2 marks. Award 1 mark for predicting that he will unlock the door.

Award 1 mark for evidence: he has been practising unlocking the schoolroom door./He has been planning this for a while./The key looked important./He wanted to know what was inside the room.

5 2 marks. Award 1 mark for identifying that Billy might be tired/no longer excited/sleepy/exhausted/sad to be leaving.

Award 1 mark for evidence that suggests he had a busy, tiring time at the beach: played in the sea; surfing; swimming; built castles; played football; pony rides; fun fair; asking 'Are we there yet?' suggests he wants to get home.

Understanding more about non-fiction (pages 39–41)

1 Could be used instead of plates/cheap/convenient.

2 1 mark for different style/different times of building.

1 mark for evidence from the text that shows a difference in style or time, e.g. the attics were Anglo-Saxon and the third floor was Norman.

3 1 mark for sustainable living or an explanation that nature and human life are linked.

1 mark for evidence: steamy jungles; waterfall; architecture; garden displays; demonstrations; rainforest canopy walkway; regeneration.

4 (gaining) mass-media attention; (generally) made headlines.

5 1 mark for two different words underlined: divides; easier (to turn); increase (speed; pedalling force; multiply; large wheels.

Understanding more about fiction (pages 43–45)

1 He told himself that they would have been horrible./He convinced himself that he didn't want them anyway.

2 They helped each other with the subjects they were not good at.

3 Because they call him names./They make up jokes about his mum which they find funny. He does not find it funny.

4 1 mark for each correct answer up to 2 marks. She shivered; until she could come out of hiding; dull pounding of her rhythmic heart; Be quiet; she whispered; should she run?; What was towering over her?; didn't dare to turn round; worst nightmare come true; Don't panic.

5 (the intentions of the Meltons) aren't purely welcoming.

Discussing language choices in fiction (pages 47–49)

1 Award 1 mark for an explanation that the night is being compared to a cocoon and an explanation of one half of this phrase: A cocoon keeps a growing/changing insect safe, warm and dry until it is time to emerge. The writer is describing that the writer feels protected because the night is wrapped around him/her to protect him/her like a cocoon protects a growing insect.

Award 2 marks for an answer that explains both halves of this phrase.

2 a) Harry's face dropped.

b) It tells you that Harry was really disappointed./The writer wants you to feel Harry's disappointment./He wants you to visualise the expression on Harry's face to let you know how disappointed/upset he was.

3 a) tick: an animal

b) Award 2 marks for identifying that this is personification and providing two examples, such as: the sea had other plans; the sea swallowed him and spat him out.

4 There was strict discipline at school. If children stepped out of line, they were not obeying the rules and would be punished. 'Teachers toughened up their pupils by hitting them …'.

5 a) 'there was hell to pay if you got caught.'

b) By suggesting the punishment was severe, the writer wants the reader to feel sorry for schoolchildren in Ancient Greece/become interested in reading on to find out what the punishment was.

6 a) 'tree-shapes crouched down'
b) It gives you the image of the trees like people crouching down and bending over.
OR a) 'One bird spoke'
b) It lets you think that the bird is speaking just like a person.
OR a) The owl is described as looking like a person 'who has been up all night'.
b) It likens the owl's appearance to a person.

Discussing language choices in poetry (pages 51–53)

1 To remind the reader of the speed at which the train is moving past objects in the countryside. / To make the reader read at a quick pace in time with the speed of the train as it moves through the countryside.

2 To make the reader feel disgusted or repulsed. The creatures tend to be things that people don't like. For example, 'toe of frog', 'Lizard's leg'. The poem is a spell intended to cause trouble / harm. It says 'a charm of powerful trouble'. Horrible creatures would make a bad spell.

3 The writer intends this to be a funny poem / humorous. It is funny because the repetition of the words 'can' and 'can-can' turn the poem into a tongue-twister / make you jumble up the words as you say them. This makes you laugh. / The lines are short so you read them quickly. Reading quickly means you will get the words mixed up which is funny.

4 By comparing Ernie to a plant / by using metaphorical language to compare Ernie to a plant: he put down roots on the settee, which means that he is settled there. / His face became a flower and his hair grew leaves. / His mother watered him and pulled weeds out of his hair.

Making comparisons (pages 55–57)

1 Award 1 mark each for identifying the writer's feelings at the beginning and at the end: The writer's feelings have changed from excitement to hatred. At the beginning the writer feels excited and happy, loving the adventure and the journey to his new home. At the end he hates the place he is in. He feels like a prisoner. / At the beginning the writer is on an adventure, feeling happy and excited. At the end, he is locked in a dormitory block like a prisoner.

2 a) Animal cells and plants cells both have cytoplasm and a nucleus.
b) Animal cells are round; plant cells are rectangular. Plant cells have a cell wall but animal cells do not. Plant cells have chloroplasts but animal cells do not.

3 a) Award 2 marks for any two of the following: Frogs have long legs for leaping and swimming. Toads have short legs for walking. / Frogs have smooth or slimy skin. Toads have warty and dry skin. / Frogs lay eggs in clusters. Toads lay eggs in long chains.
b) They both lay eggs.

4 a) European dragons are often winged. Chinese dragons resemble large snakes.
b) Award 2 marks for any two of the following: They are portrayed as serpentine or reptilian; hatch from eggs and possess scaly or feathered bodies; breathe fire or are poisonous.

5 2 marks: Zach is older and taller than Willie.